T0068145

A is for Abraham!

Coloring Journal with Bible Scriptures

Lavonia Lonzo, EdD

authorHOUSE

AuthorHouse™
1663 Liberty Drive
Bloomington, IN 47403
www.authorhouse.com
Phone: 833-262-8899

Published by AuthorHouse 06/18/2021

ISBN: 978-1-6655-2610-4 (sc)
ISBN: 978-1-6655-2635-7 (e)

Print information available on the last page.

This book is printed on acid-free paper.

Scripture quotations marked KJV are from the Holy Bible, King James Version (Authorized Version). First published in 1611. Quoted from the KJV Classic Reference Bible, Copyright © 1983 by The Zondervan Corporation.

To my grandchildren:
Andrew, Elijah, and Hannah.
Love the LORD!

Purpose

The **A is for Abraham Coloring Journal** inspires God's children of all ages to learn more about the Bible. It sparks interest about Biblical concepts, people, places, and events. It builds moral character and understanding about the LORD. This hands-on learning tool is engaging and supports the development of reading skills.

Children can learn sight words such as: the, it, is, and for, as well as, vocabulary, comprehension, and fluency using keywords and illustrations while learning their colors! It can also be used to memorize scriptures and increase the understanding of them. After the journal is completed, it can be a keepsake and shared with the next generation!

Evangelist Lavonia Lonzo, EdD

THIS JOURNAL BELONGS TO:

Name: _____

Date: _____

Age: _____

From: _____with Love!

Sight Word
Assessment Tool

There are a set of questions for each illustration and they are primarily composed of sight words.

Point to each sight word while reading the questions and use the illustrations and scriptures to find the answers to each of the questions or the questions can be read aloud for verbal answers.

Have Fun!

Can you tell me if fire is hot or cold?

Aa is for Abraham

Genesis 17:5

Neither shall thy name any more be called Abram, but thy name shall be Abraham; for the father of many nations have I made thee.

What do you think this is called?

Bb is for Babel

Genesis 11:9

Therefore, is the name of it called Babel; because the LORD did there confound the language of all the earth: and from thence did the LORD scatter them abroad upon the face of all the earth.

Can you tell me the name of this place?

Cc is for Calvary

What do you think the boy tore out of his bag?

Luke 23:33

And when they were come to the place, which is called Calvary, there they crucified him, and the malefactors, one on the right hand, and the other on the left.

What do you think the boy took out of his bag?

Dd is for David

I Samuel 17:49

And David put his hand in his bag, and took thence a stone, and slang it, and smote the Philistine in his forehead, that the stone sunk into his forehead; and he fell upon his face to the earth.

Can you tell me the baby's name?

Ee is for Emmanuel

Who do you think is holding the baby's hand in this picture?

Matthew 1:23

Behold, a virgin shall be with child, and shall bring forth a son, and they shall call his name Emmanuel, which being interpreted is, God with us.

Who do you think is holding the baby's hand in this picture?

Ff is for Father

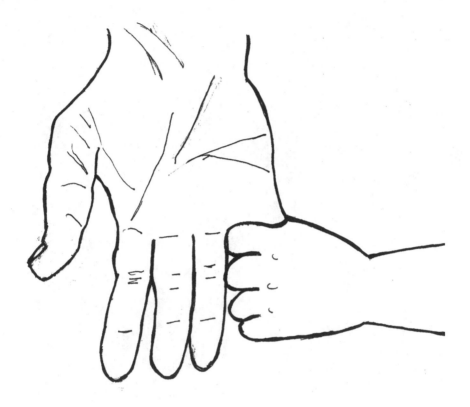

John 14:2

In my Father's house are many mansions: if it were not so, I would have told you. I go to prepare a place for you.

Do you think the earth is big or small?

Gg is for God

Genesis 1:1

In the beginning God created the heaven and the earth.

What do you think can go up in the air in this picture?

Hh is for Holy Ghost

Romans 14:17

For the kingdom of God is not meat and drink; but righteousness, and peace, and joy in the Holy Ghost.

Can you tell me the name of this place?

Ii is for Israel

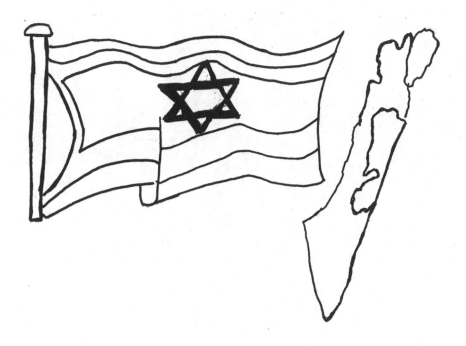

Matthew 2:21

And he arose, and took the young child and his mother, and came into the land of Israel.

Can you tell me the baby's name?

Jj is for Jesus

Matthew 1:21

And she shall bring forth a son, and thou shalt call his name Jᴇsus: for he shall save his people from their sins.

What do you think a king wears on his head?

Kk is for King

Psalm 47:7

For God is the King of all the earth: sing ye praises with understanding.

Can you tell me how many lambs you see?

Ll is for Lambs

Proverbs 27:26

The lambs are for thy clothing, and the goats are the price of the field.

Who do you think the people came to see in this picture?

Mm is for Mary

Luke 2:16

And they came with haste, and found Mary, and Joseph, and the babe lying in a manger.

Can you tell me the man's name in this picture?

Nn is for Noah

Genesis 7:15

And they went in unto Noah into the ark, two and two of all flesh, wherein is the breath of life.

Can you tell me what you see in this picture?

Oo is for Overcomer

OVERCOMER

Romans 12:21

Be not overcome of evil, but overcome evil with good.

What do you think this man's name is in this picture?

Pp is for Peter

Matthew 16:18

And I say unto thee, that thou art Peter, and upon this rock I will build my church; and the gates of hell shall not prevail against it.

Can you tell me how many birds do you see in this picture?

Qq is for Quails

Psalm 105:40

The people asked, and he brought quails, and satisfied them with the bread of heaven.

Which one of the ladies in this picture is Ruth?

Rr is for Ruth

Ruth 1:16

And Ruth said, intreat me not to leave thee, or to return from following after thee: for whither thou goest, I will go; and where thou lodgest, I will lodge: thy people shall be my people and thy God my God.

Do you think the person in this picture is weak or strong?

Ss is for Strong

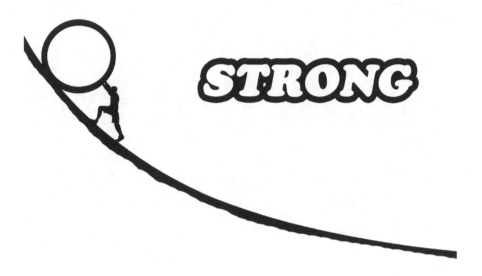

Ephesians 6:10

Finally, my brethren, be strong in the Lord, and in the power of his might.

Who do you think is Timothy in this picture?

Tt is for Timothy

Hebrews 13:23

Know ye that our brother Timothy is set at liberty; with whom, if he comes shortly, I will see you.

What do you think this animal is called?

Uu is for Unicorn

Psalm 29:6

He maketh them also to skip like a calf; Lebanon and Sirion like a young unicorn.

Do you think this picture is about winning or losing?

Vv is for Victory

I Corinthians 15:57

But thanks be to God, which giveth us the victory through our Lord Jesus Christ.

Can you tell me what you see in this picture?

Ww is for Wheels

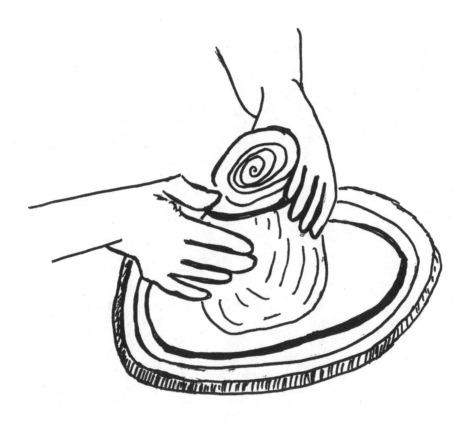

Jeremiah 18:3

Then I went down to the potter's house, and,
behold, he wrought a work on the wheels.

What is the man's name in this picture?

Xx is for eXcellent

Daniel 6:3

Then this Daniel was preferred above the presidents and princes, because an excellent spirit was in him; and the king thought to set him over the whole realm.

What do you think the children are doing in this picture?

Yy is for Youth

Ecclesiastes 12:1

Remember now thy Creator in the days of thy youth, while the evil days come not, nor the years draw nigh, when thou shalt say, I have no pleasure in them;

Who do you think this could be in the tree?

Zz is for Zacchaeus

Luke 19:5

And when Jesus came to the place, he looked up, and saw him, and said unto him, Zacchaeus, make haste, and come down; for today I must abide at thy house.

BIBLE TOPICS WITH SCRIPTURES

THE BIBLE
THE FIRST FAMILY
SIN
CAIN AND ABEL
NOAH
RUTH
THE LORD'S PRAYER
I CORINTHIANS 13
SALVATION
GOD'S LOVE
THE BEATITUDES
FAITH
PSALM 23
ISAIAH 53:1-7
1 THESSALONIANS 4:11-18
JUDE 20-25

THE BIBLE

John 1:1

In the beginning was the Word, and the Word was with God, and the Word was God.

Psalm 119:11

Thy word have I hid in mine heart, that I might not sin against thee.

Psalm 119:89

Forever, O Lord, thy word is settled in heaven.

Psalm 119:105

Thy word is a lamp unto my feet, and a light unto my path.

Mark 13:31-32

[31] Heaven and earth shall pass away: but my words shall not pass away. [32] But of that day and that hour knoweth no man, no, not the angels which are in heaven, neither the Son, but the Father.

THE FIRST FAMILY

Genesis 2:7

And the Lord God formed man of the dust of the ground and breathed into his nostrils the breath of life; and man became a living soul.

Genesis 1:27

So, God created man in his own image, in the image of God created he him; male and female created he them.

Mark 10:6

But from the beginning of the creation God made them male and female.

Genesis 2:24

Therefore, shall a man leave his father and his mother, and shall cleave unto his wife: and they shall be one flesh.

SIN

Genesis 3:1-6

Now the serpent was more subtle than any beast of the field which the Lord God had made. And he said unto the woman, Yea, hath God said, Ye shall not eat of every tree of the garden?

2 And the woman said unto the serpent, we may eat of the fruit of the trees of the garden:

3 But of the fruit of the tree which is in the midst of the garden, God hath said, Ye shall not eat of it, neither shall ye touch it, lest ye die.

4 And the serpent said unto the woman, Ye shall not surely die:

5 For God doth know that in the day ye eat thereof, then your eyes shall be opened, and ye shall be as gods, knowing good and evil.

6 And when the woman saw that the tree was good for food, and that it was pleasant to the eyes, and a tree to be desired to make one wise, she took of the fruit thereof, and did eat, and gave also unto her husband with her; and he did eat.

SIN

Genesis 3:8-9

8 And they heard the voice of the Lord God walking in the garden in the cool of the day: and Adam and his wife hid themselves from the presence of the Lord God amongst the trees of the garden.

9 And the Lord God called unto Adam, and said unto him, Where art thou?

Genesis 3:12-14

12 And the man said, the woman whom thou gavest to be with me, she gave me of the tree, and I did eat.

13 And the Lord God said unto the woman, What is this that thou hast done? And the woman said, the serpent beguiled me, and I did eat.

14 And the Lord God said unto the serpent, because thou hast done this, thou art cursed above all cattle, and above every beast of the field; upon thy belly shalt thou go, and dust shalt thou eat all the days of thy life.

SIN

Genesis 3:15-19

[15] And I will put enmity between thee and the woman, and between thy seed and her seed; it shall bruise thy head, and thou shalt bruise his heel.

[16] Unto the woman he said, I will greatly multiply thy sorrow and thy conception; in sorrow thou shalt bring forth children; and thy desire shall be to thy husband, and he shall rule over thee.

[17] And unto Adam he said, because thou hast hearkened unto the voice of thy wife, and hast eaten of the tree, of which I commanded thee, saying, Thou shalt not eat of it: cursed is the ground for thy sake; in sorrow shalt thou eat of it all the days of thy life;

[18] Thorns also and thistles shall it bring forth to thee; and thou shalt eat the herb of the field;

[19] In the sweat of thy face shalt thou eat bread, till thou return unto the ground; for out of it wast thou taken: for dust thou art, and unto dust shalt thou return.

CAIN AND ABEL

Genesis 4:1-8

[1] And Adam knew Eve his wife; and she conceived, and bare Cain, and said, I have gotten a man from the Lord. [2] And she again bare his brother Abel. And Abel was a keeper of sheep, but Cain was a tiller of the ground.

[3] And in process of time it came to pass, that Cain brought of the fruit of the ground an offering unto the Lord. [4] And Abel, he also brought of the firstlings of his flock and of the fat thereof. And the Lord had respect unto Abel and to his offering:

[5] But unto Cain and to his offering he had not respect. And Cain was very wroth, and his countenance fell.

[6] And the Lord said unto Cain, Why art thou wroth? And why is thy countenance fallen?

[7] If thou doest well, shalt thou not be accepted? And if thou doest not well, sin lieth at the door. And unto thee shall be his desire, and thou shalt rule over him.

[8] And Cain talked with Abel his brother: and it came to pass, when they were in the field, that Cain rose up against Abel his brother, and slew him.

NOAH

Genesis 5:32

[32] And Noah was five hundred years old: and Noah begat Shem, Ham, and Japheth.

Genesis 6:12-15

[12] And God looked upon the earth, and, behold, it was corrupt; for all flesh had corrupted his way upon the earth.

[13] And God said unto Noah, the end of all flesh is come before me; for the earth is filled with violence through them; and, behold, I will destroy them with the earth.

[14] Make thee an ark of gopher wood; rooms shalt thou make in the ark, and shalt pitch it within and without with pitch.

[15] And this is the fashion which thou shalt make it of: The length of the ark shall be three hundred cubits, the breadth of it fifty cubits, and the height of it thirty cubits.

NOAH

Genesis 6:16-19

¹⁶ A window shalt thou make to the ark, and in a cubit shalt thou finish it above; and the door of the ark shalt thou set in the side thereof; with lower, second, and third stories shalt thou make it.

¹⁷ And, behold, I, even I, do bring a flood of waters upon the earth, to destroy all flesh, wherein is the breath of life, from under heaven; and everything that is in the earth shall die.

¹⁸ But with thee will I establish my covenant; and thou shalt come into the ark, thou, and thy sons, and thy wife, and thy sons' wives with thee.

¹⁹ And of every living thing of all flesh, two of every sort shalt thou bring into the ark, to keep them alive with thee; they shall be male and female.

NOAH

Genesis 7:1-4

¹ And the Lord said unto Noah, come thou and all thy house into the ark; for thee have I seen righteous before me in this generation.

² Of every clean beast thou shalt take to thee by sevens, the male and his female: and of beasts that are not clean by two, the male and his female.

³ Of fowls also of the air by sevens, the male and the female; to keep seed alive upon the face of all the earth.

⁴ For yet seven days, and I will cause it to rain upon the earth forty days and forty nights; and every living substance that I have made will I destroy from off the face of the earth.

NOAH

Genesis 7:5-10

⁵ And Noah did according unto all that the Lord commanded him.

⁶ And Noah was six hundred years old when the flood of waters was upon the earth.

⁷ And Noah went in, and his sons, and his wife, and his sons' wives with him, into the ark, because of the waters of the flood.

⁸ Of clean beasts, and of beasts that are not clean, and of fowls, and of everything that creepeth upon the earth,

⁹ There went in two and two unto Noah into the ark, the male and the female, as God had commanded Noah.

¹⁰ And it came to pass after seven days, that the waters of the flood were upon the earth.

NOAH

Genesis 7:12-17

¹² And the rain was upon the earth forty days and forty nights.

¹³ In the selfsame day entered Noah, and Shem, and Ham, and Japheth, the sons of Noah, and Noah's wife, and the three wives of his sons with them, into the ark;

¹⁴ They, and every beast after his kind, and all the cattle after their kind, and every creeping thing that creepeth upon the earth after his kind, and every fowl after his kind, every bird of every sort.

¹⁵ And they went in unto Noah into the ark, two and two of all flesh, wherein is the breath of life.

¹⁶ And they that went in, went in male and female of all flesh, as God had commanded him: and the Lord shut him in.

¹⁷ And the flood was forty days upon the earth; and the waters increased, and bare up the ark, and it was lift up above the earth.

NOAH

Genesis 7:23-24

²³ And every living substance was destroyed which was upon the face of the ground, both man, and cattle, and the creeping things, and the fowl of the heaven; and they were destroyed from the earth: and Noah only remained alive, and they that were with him in the ark.²⁴ And the waters prevailed upon the earth an hundred and fifty days.

Genesis 9:1-3

¹And God blessed Noah and his sons, and said unto them, Be fruitful, and multiply, and replenish the earth.

² And the fear of you and the dread of you shall be upon every beast of the earth, and upon every fowl of the air, upon all that moveth upon the earth, and upon all the fishes of the sea; into your hand are they delivered.

³ Every moving thing that liveth shall be meat for you; even as the green herb have I given you all things.

NOAH

Genesis 9:4-9

[4] But flesh with the life thereof, which is the blood thereof, shall ye not eat.

[5] And surely your blood of your lives will I require; at the hand of every beast will I require it, and at the hand of man; at the hand of every man's brother will I require the life of man.

[6] Whoso sheddeth man's blood, by man shall his blood be shed: for in the image of God made he man.

[7] And you, be ye fruitful, and multiply; bring forth abundantly in the earth, and multiply therein.

[8] And God spake unto Noah, and to his sons with him, saying,

[9] And I, behold, I establish my covenant with you, and with your seed after you;

NOAH

Genesis 9:10-14

[10] And with every living creature that is with you, of the fowl, of the cattle, and of every beast of the earth with you; from all that go out of the ark, to every beast of the earth.

[11] And I will establish my covenant with you, neither shall all flesh be cut off any more by the waters of a flood; neither shall there anymore be a flood to destroy the earth.

[12] And God said, this is the token of the covenant which I make between me and you and every living creature that is with you, for perpetual generations:

[13] I do set my bow in the cloud, and it shall be for a token of a covenant between me and the earth.

[14] And it shall come to pass, when I bring a cloud over the earth, that the bow shall be seen in the cloud: [15] And I will remember my covenant, which is between me and you and every living creature of all flesh; and the waters shall no more become a flood to destroy all flesh.

RUTH

Ruth 1:1-4

[1]Now it came to pass in the days when the judges ruled, that there was a famine in the land. And a certain man of Bethlehemjudah went to sojourn in the country of Moab, he, and his wife, and his two sons.

[2] And the name of the man was Elimelech, and the name of his wife Naomi, and the name of his two sons Mahlon and Chilion, Ephrathites of Bethlehemjudah. And they came into the country of Moab, and continued there.

[3] And Elimelech Naomi's husband died; and she was left, and her two sons.

[4] And they took them wives of the women of Moab; the name of the one was Orpah, and the name of the other Ruth: and they dwelled there about ten years.

RUTH

Ruth 1:5-8

⁵ And Mahlon and Chilion died also both of them; and the woman was left of her two sons and her husband.

⁶ Then she arose with her daughters in law, that she might return from the country of Moab: for she had heard in the country of Moab how that the Lord had visited his people in giving them bread.

⁷ Wherefore she went forth out of the place where she was, and her two daughters in law with her; and they went on the way to return unto the land of Judah.

⁸ And Naomi said unto her two daughters in law, Go, return each to her mother's house: the Lord deal kindly with you, as ye have dealt with the dead, and with me.

RUTH

Ruth 1:9-13

[9] The Lord grant you that ye may find rest, each of you in the house of her husband. Then she kissed them; and they lifted up their voice, and wept.

[10] And they said unto her, Surely we will return with thee unto thy people.

[11] And Naomi said, Turn again, my daughters: why will ye go with me? are there yet any more sons in my womb, that they may be your husbands?

[12] Turn again, my daughters, go your way; for I am too old to have an husband. If I should say, I have hope, if I should have an husband also to night, and should also bear sons;

[13] Would ye tarry for them till they were grown? would ye stay for them from having husbands? nay, my daughters; for it grieveth me much for your sakes that the hand of the Lord is gone out against me.

RUTH

Ruth 1:14-18

[14] And they lifted up their voice, and wept again: and Orpah kissed her mother in law; but Ruth clave unto her.

[15] And she said, Behold, thy sister in law is gone back unto her people, and unto her gods: return thou after thy sister in law.

[16] And Ruth said, Intreat me not to leave thee, or to return from following after thee: for whither thou goest, I will go; and where thou lodgest, I will lodge: thy people shall be my people, and thy God my God:

[17] Where thou diest, will I die, and there will I be buried: the Lord do so to me, and more also, if ought but death part thee and me.

[18] When she saw that she was stedfastly minded to go with her, then she left speaking unto her.

THE LORD'S PRAYER

Matthew 6:9-15

[9] After this manner therefore pray ye: Our Father which art in heaven, Hallowed be thy name.

[10] Thy kingdom come, thy will be done in earth, as it is in heaven.

[11] Give us this day our daily bread.

[12] And forgive us our debts, as we forgive our debtors.

[13] And lead us not into temptation, but deliver us from evil: For thine is the kingdom, and the power, and the glory, forever. Amen.

[14] For if ye forgive men their trespasses, your heavenly Father will also forgive you:

[15] But if ye forgive not men their trespasses, neither will your Father forgive your trespasses.

I CORINTIANS 13

I Corinthians 13:1-6

[21] Though I speak with the tongues of men and of angels, and have not charity, I am become as sounding brass, or a tinkling cymbal.

[2] And though I have the gift of prophecy, and understand all mysteries, and all knowledge; and though I have all faith, so that I could remove mountains, and have not charity, I am nothing.

[3] And though I bestow all my goods to feed the poor, and though I give my body to be burned, and have not charity, it profiteth me nothing.

[4] Charity suffereth long, and is kind; charity envieth not; charity vaunteth not itself, is not puffed up,

[5] Doth not behave itself unseemly, seeketh not her own, is not easily provoked, thinketh no evil;

[6] Rejoiceth not in iniquity, but rejoiceth in the truth;

I CORINTHIANS 13

I Corinthians 13:7-13

[7] Beareth all things, believeth all things, hopeth all things, endureth all things.

[8] Charity never faileth: but whether there be prophecies, they shall fail; whether there be tongues, they shall cease; whether there be knowledge, it shall vanish away. [9] For we know in part, and we prophesy in part.

[10] But when that which is perfect is come, then that which is in part shall be done away.

[11] When I was a child, I spake as a child, I understood as a child, I thought as a child: but when I became a man, I put away childish things.

[12] For now we see through a glass, darkly; but then face to face: now I know in part; but then shall I know even as also I am known.

[13] And now abideth faith, hope, charity, these three; but the greatest of these is charity.

SALVATION

Matthew 18:1-3

[1]At the same time came the disciples unto Jesus, saying, Who is the greatest in the kingdom of heaven?

[2] And Jesus called a little child unto him, and set him in the midst of them,

[3] And said, Verily I say unto you, Except ye be converted, and become as little children, ye shall not enter into the kingdom of heaven.

Romans 10:9-10

[9] That if thou shalt confess with thy mouth the Lord Jesus, and shalt believe in thine heart that God hath raised him from the dead, thou shalt be saved.

[10] For with the heart man believeth unto righteousness; and with the mouth confession is made unto salvation.

GOD'S LOVE

John 3:16-20

[16] For God so loved the world, that he gave his only begotten Son, that whosoever believeth in him should not perish, but have everlasting life.

[17] For God sent not his Son into the world to condemn the world; but that the world through him might be saved.

[18] He that believeth on him is not condemned: but he that believeth not is condemned already, because he hath not believed in the name of the only begotten Son of God.

[19] And this is the condemnation, that light is come into the world, and men loved darkness rather than light, because their deeds were evil.

[20] For everyone that doeth evil hateth the light, neither cometh to the light, lest his deeds should be reproved.

GOD'S LOVE

1 John 4:7

Beloved, let us love one another: for love is of God; and everyone that loveth is born of God, and knoweth God.

1 John 4:8

He that loveth not knoweth not God; for God is love.

1 John 4:10

Herein is love, not that we loved God, but that he loved us, and sent his Son to be the propitiation for our sins.

THE BEATITUDES

Matthew 5:2-11

[2] And he opened his mouth, and taught them, saying, [3] Blessed are the poor in spirit: for theirs is the kingdom of heaven. [4] Blessed are they that mourn: for they shall be comforted.

[5] Blessed are the meek: for they shall inherit the earth.

[6] Blessed are they which do hunger and thirst after righteousness: for they shall be filled. [7] Blessed are the merciful: for they shall obtain mercy.

[8] Blessed are the pure in heart: for they shall see God. [9] Blessed are the peacemakers: for they shall be called the children of God. [10] Blessed are they which are persecuted for righteousness' sake: for theirs is the kingdom of heaven.

[11] Blessed are ye, when men shall revile you, and persecute you, and shall say all manner of evil against you falsely, for my sake.

FAITH

Luke 17:5

And the apostles said unto the Lord, Increase our faith.

Hebrews 11:6

But without faith it is impossible to please him: for he that cometh to God must believe that he is, and that he is a rewarder of them that diligently seek him.

Romans 1:17

For therein is the righteousness of God revealed from faith to faith: as it is written, the just shall live by faith.

PSALM 23

Psalm 23:1-6

[1] The Lord is my shepherd; I shall not want.

[2] He maketh me to lie down in green pastures: he leadeth me beside the still waters.

[3] He restoreth my soul: he leadeth me in the paths of righteousness for his name's sake.

[4] Yea, though I walk through the valley of the shadow of death, I will fear no evil: for thou art with me; thy rod and thy staff they comfort me.

[5] Thou preparest a table before me in the presence of mine enemies: thou anointest my head with oil; my cup runneth over.

[6] Surely goodness and mercy shall follow me all the days of my life: and I will dwell in the house of the Lord forever.

ISAIAH 53

Isaiah 53:1-7

[1] Who hath believed our report? and to whom is the arm of the Lord revealed? [2] For he shall grow up before him as a tender plant, and as a root out of a dry ground: he hath no form nor comeliness; and when we shall see him, there is no beauty that we should desire him.

[3] He is despised and rejected of men; a man of sorrows, and acquainted with grief: and we hid as it were our faces from him; he was despised, and we esteemed him not.

[4] Surely he hath borne our griefs, and carried our sorrows: yet we did esteem him stricken, smitten of God, and afflicted.

[5] But he was wounded for our transgressions, he was bruised for our iniquities: the chastisement of our peace was upon him; and with his stripes we are healed.

[6] All we like sheep have gone astray; we have turned everyone to his own way; and the Lord hath laid on him the iniquity of us all.

[7] He was oppressed, and he was afflicted, yet he opened not his mouth: he is brought as a lamb to the slaughter, and as a sheep before her shearers is dumb, so he openeth not his mouth.

I THESSALONIANS

I Thessalonians 4:11-18

[11] And that ye study to be quiet, and to do your own business, and to work with your own hands, as we commanded you;

[12] That ye may walk honestly toward them that are without, and that ye may have lack of nothing.

[13] But I would not have you to be ignorant, brethren, concerning them which are asleep, that ye sorrow not, even as others which have no hope.

[14] For if we believe that Jesus died and rose again, even so them also which sleep in Jesus will God bring with him.

[15] For this we say unto you by the word of the Lord, that we which are alive and remain unto the coming of the Lord shall not prevent them which are asleep.

[16] For the Lord himself shall descend from heaven with a shout, with the voice of the archangel, and with the trump of God: and the dead in Christ shall rise first:

[17] Then we which are alive and remain shall be caught up together with them in the clouds, to meet the Lord in the air: and so shall we ever be with the Lord. [18] Wherefore comfort one another with these words.

JUDE

Jude 20-25

[20] But ye, beloved, building up yourselves on your most holy faith, praying in the Holy Ghost,

[21] Keep yourselves in the love of God, looking for the mercy of our Lord Jesus Christ unto eternal life.

[22] And of some have compassion, making a difference:

[23] And others save with fear, pulling them out of the fire; hating even the garment spotted by the flesh.

[24] Now unto him that is able to keep you from falling, and to present you faultless before the presence of his glory with exceeding joy,

[25] To the only wise God our Saviour, be glory and majesty, dominion and power, both now and ever. Amen.